Where Is Indiana?

Where Is Indiana?

by Tracy Vonder Brink

illustrated by Ted Hammond

Penguin Workshop

For the state where I was born and raised—TVB

PENGUIN WORKSHOP
An imprint of Penguin Random House LLC
1745 Broadway, New York, NY 10019
penguinrandomhouse.com

Designed and Produced by Dinardo Design, LLC.

Library of Congress Cataloging-in-Publication Data is available.

First published in the United States of America by Penguin Workshop, 2026

Manufactured in the United States of America
CJKW

ISBN 9798217243372 (paperback)
10 9 8 7 6 5 4 3 2 1

ISBN 9798217243389 (library binding)
10 9 8 7 6 5 4 3 2 1

The authorized representative in the EU for product safety and compliance is Penguin Random House Ireland, Morrison Chambers, 32 Nassau Street, Dublin D02 YH68, Ireland, https://eu-contact.penguin.ie.

Contents

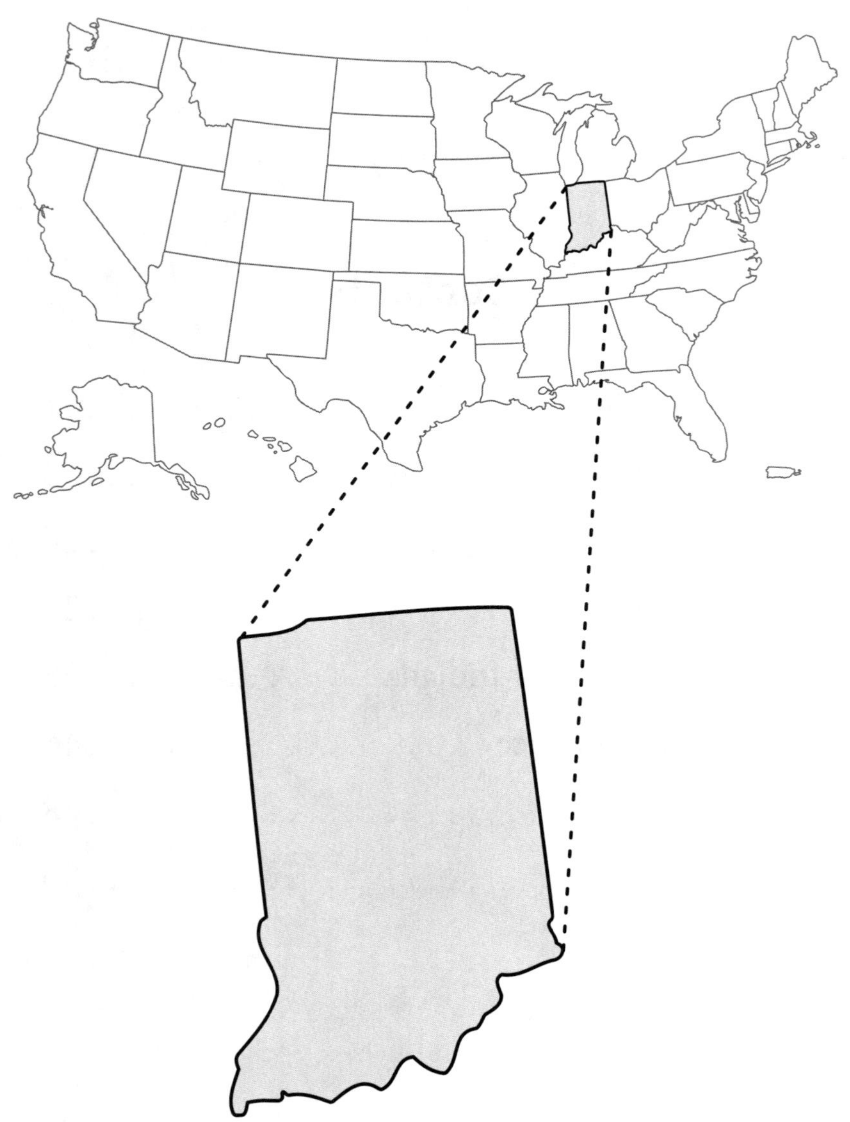

Where Is Indiana?

A cannon thunders over the Indianapolis Motor Speedway. It's race day! Hundreds of thousands of excited fans fill the stands. Roger Penske, the speedway's chairman, steps up to a microphone. His voice rings out: "Drivers, start your engines!" The crowd roars as thirty-three race cars roll out. Cars circle the track to warm up. A green flag is waved. The cars take off!

Engines hum like a swarm of bees as the drivers push their cars to speeds of 190 miles per hour or more. They go two hundred laps around the track, equaling five hundred miles. The drivers fight to pass each other and stay in front. The smallest mistake can cause a crash. And in the end, there can only be one winner.

This race is the Indianapolis 500, sometimes

called the Indy 500. It's held every year, usually around Memorial Day. Fifty-one American drivers have won it.

The Indy 500 has been held for more than one hundred years. It's a unique tradition that makes people proud to live in Indiana, but it's not the only one.

CHAPTER 1
Welcome to Indiana

Indiana's total land area is 35,825 square miles, making it the thirty-eighth largest US state. Indiana is almost twice as long as it is wide. The state is bordered by Michigan and Lake Michigan to the north. Kentucky lies to its south. Ohio is to its east and Illinois its west.

The northern and central parts of the state are covered with large areas of flat land called plains. More than fifteen thousand years ago, a glacier (a huge area of ice that stays frozen for hundreds or even thousands of years) flowed down from the north. Its heavy weight flattened two-thirds of what became Indiana and created its plains. When the glacier melted, it left behind rivers and lakes. Most of the other land in what would become Indiana was covered in hardwood trees including oaks and maples. Flowering varieties such as tulip trees also filled the forests.

Larger mammals such as deer share the land with smaller animals such as moles and shrews. Indiana's wetlands, mostly along rivers and lakes, are home to more common birds such as swans and ducks as well as the sandhill crane. The sandhill crane is one of the oldest bird species on

the planet. Every year, thousands migrate through wetlands in Medaryville.

The glacier also dropped materials that became Indiana's rich soil. No other state has as much good land for farming. Much of Indiana is now cleared of forest for farming. Indiana's mild climate means crops can grow up to six months out of the year. Summer highs reach eighty degrees, while winter lows are usually around twenty-five

degrees. The state also gets plenty of rain—about three feet of rain falls on the northern part of the state every year, and the south sees almost four!

The first people to reach the land that became Indiana arrived around 10,000 BCE. They lived near water and used stone tools to hunt. Over thousands of years, their relatives spread through Indiana. Mississippian culture is the term used to describe groups of people who lived in the midwestern and southeastern United States from around 800 to 1600 CE. We don't know what they called themselves, but they were probably made up of many nations.

Between 1050 and 1450, one of these nations built a city on the Ohio River near what is now Evansville. As many as one thousand people lived and worked there. The city covered hundreds of acres and included eleven mounds built out of earth. Homes for important leaders may have been on top of some of them. Other mounds were sacred gathering places. We don't know exactly why, but the city was abandoned after about three hundred years. Today, this historic site is known as Angel Mounds.

Other Indigenous nations later moved into what became Indiana. The Miami Nation built communities near what is now Fort Wayne. The Potawatomi Nation made their homes around the southern shores of Lake Michigan. The Shawnee, Lenape (say: lun-NAH-pay), Kickapoo, and other nations also lived across the state. These peoples were part of the Algonquian (say: al-GON-kwee-uhn) culture, although each had its own traditions and languages.

The first Europeans to arrive in the late 1600s were French fur traders. By 1763, England controlled the territory. When the American Revolution began in 1775, with the thirteen colonies fighting for independence from Britain, George Rogers Clark volunteered to force British soldiers out of the Ohio Valley. (That area contained part of what is now Indiana.) In 1779, Clark led a small volunteer army against a British fort at Vincennes. He and his men marched for eighteen days and crossed flooded streams in water up to their shoulders. At the fort, Clark fooled the British into thinking he had an army of a thousand men. The British surrendered after two days of fighting. Clark's victory gave the

Americans control of the entire Ohio Valley.

When the Revolutionary War ended, England gave the land west of the Appalachian Mountains to the United States, even though Indigenous nations already lived there. In Indiana, the Miami Nation—who call themselves Myaamia (say: me-AH-me-ya)—had a capital village near the St. Joseph and Maumee Rivers. It was called Kekionga (say: kee-kee-ON-ga). In spring, members of the

Miami, Huron, Ottawa, and Shawnee Nations gathered in Kekionga to trade and plant crops. They also met there to discuss how to protect their lands and people from American settlers.

In 1790, President George Washington ordered American soldiers to attack Kekionga. General Josiah Harmar and his soldiers fought

Chief Little Turtle of the Miami, called Mihšihkinaahkwa (say: mish-eh-kin-AW-kwa) by his people, and his men. The Battle of Kekionga was the first battle the US Army fought after the Revolutionary War. The Americans lost.

Little Turtle and his men won more battles over the next year. In 1794, they met the US Army at the Battle of Fallen Timbers in what is now Ohio. This time, the Americans, led by General Anthony Wayne, won. The peace agreement that followed ended the Indigenous nations' fight against the United States. Wayne returned to where the Battle of Kekionga had been fought to build a fort. He named it after himself. Later, the city of Fort Wayne was founded where the fort once stood.

In 1800, the US government made Indiana a territory. William Henry Harrison became the territorial governor. He encouraged the US Congress to pass the Harrison Land Act of 1800, which made land cheaper. At that time, most of Indiana was still Indigenous land. Harrison was given the job of forcing Indigenous nations to sign agreements giving it up. Many of these agreements were signed after Harrison sent American soldiers to defeat Indigenous nations in battle. From 1803 to 1809, the agreements Harrison made took millions of acres of land from Indigenous peoples, including much of southern Indiana.

In 1808, Shawnee brothers Tenskwatawa (say: tens-kwa-TAH-wa) and Tecumseh (say: teh-CUM-suh) built a village near what is now Lafayette. Tecumseh was a great leader and fighter, and Tenskwatawa was a religious leader known as The Prophet. Their village was called Prophet's Town. The brothers wanted it to be a gathering place for members of the Shawnee, Kickapoo, Potawatomi, and other nations fighting back against the United States' violence.

In 1811, while Tecumseh was away, William Henry Harrison marched one thousand soldiers to attack Prophet's Town. The Americans fought Tenskwatawa's men at the Battle of Tippecanoe. The Americans won. Tenskwatawa escaped to Canada. After the battle, Harrison's soldiers burned Prophet's Town to the ground.

Later, the US government passed an act giving them the right to remove Indigenous nations by force. The Potawatomi Nation signed an agreement giving up their Indiana land, but more than eight hundred members refused to leave. The US Army forced them to walk from Indiana to Kansas. Forty-two people died along the way, mostly the very young and the old. This became known as the Potawatomi Trail of Death. Removing the Potawatomi and other Indigenous nations from Indiana meant that there was even more territory for American settlement.

CHAPTER 2
Becoming Hoosiers

By 1815, more than sixty thousand settlers lived in the Indiana territory. The local government felt it was ready to become a state. Meetings were held in Corydon, the territorial capital, to write a state constitution. The US Congress and President James Madison approved it. Indiana became the nineteenth state on December 11, 1816!

Indiana needed a capital city. The state government decided to build a new city for its capital and put it close to the middle of the state. To name it, they combined "Indiana" with *polis*, the Greek word for city. Building began in 1821, and Indianapolis officially became the capital in 1825. Around a year later, a road from the capital to Lake Michigan was built. The Michigan Road was one of the state's first highways. Cars still drive it today.

The US Congress allowed Indiana to set aside land for a college when it became a state. In 1820, the state chose Bloomington as the site of its first college. Building began two years later, and it opened in 1825. Its first class had only ten students! Indiana College was renamed Indiana University in 1838.

Indiana's new constitution also outlawed slavery. Many free Black pioneers moved to the state. The Beech Settlement was one of at least thirty Black farm communities founded during this time. By 1850, more than three hundred people lived in Beech Settlement. Its farms covered 2,100 acres. The settlement no longer exists, but every year the relatives of its pioneering residents gather at its historic church to celebrate their ancestors.

Even though slavery was illegal in the state,

laws still limited the rights of Black people in Indiana. They could not vote, and Black children were not allowed to attend public schools. Although Indiana's constitution said slavery was illegal, it did not free everyone who was already enslaved when it was written. In 1820, Polly Strong, who was enslaved in Vincennes, went to court to argue that she should be free. The Indiana Supreme Court agreed. Another woman named Mary Clark also sued and won. These cases gave other enslaved people in Indiana a way to fight for their freedom.

Around this time, people who lived in Indiana began to call themselves "Hoosiers" (say: WHO-zhers). The word first appeared in a letter written to an Indiana newspaper in 1831, but it was probably used even earlier. In 1833, a popular poem about Indiana pioneers spread the nickname to the rest of the country. Today, people who live in the state proudly call themselves Hoosiers,

even though nobody knows exactly where the name came from!

In the 1830s, the first highway built by the US government reached the state. Indiana's part of the National Road started in Richmond, went through Indianapolis, and ended at the Illinois border. The National Road not only helped Hoosiers travel through the state but also became an important route for settlers heading west. The state motto became "The Crossroads of America" thanks to routes like the National Road.

Hoosier farmers cleared six million acres of trees to plant crops and raise animals. By the 1850s, Indiana was one of the nation's top five producers of corn and pigs. In 1852, the first Indiana State Fair was held in Indianapolis as an event where farmers could come together. It lasted three days and attracted thirty thousand people. The Indiana State Fair has been held ever since!

Indiana became a crossroads for more than settlers in the years leading up to the Civil War. At that time, any freedom seekers captured while trying to escape slavery were enslaved again, even if they were in a state where slavery was outlawed. Some Hoosiers who were against slavery joined the Underground Railroad, the network of safe houses and secret routes that helped people reach safety in Canada. Levi Coffin and his wife Catherine lived in Fountain City. They helped so many freedom seekers that their home became known as the "Grand Central Station of the Underground Railroad." Free Black Hoosiers also played important roles. Chapman Harris was a Baptist minister and a blacksmith. He and his sons guided freedom seekers across the Ohio River. When Harris was ready to cross the river, he hammered an anvil as a signal that he was coming to help.

Abraham Lincoln became president in 1861.

He felt slavery was wrong and had spoken out against it. When he was elected, the Southern states didn't want a president who was antislavery, so they left the United States to form their own country. It was called the Confederate States of America, or the Confederacy. The US government fought to make these states stay, and the Civil War began on April 12, 1861.

Indiana joined the US government's side, called the Union. More than 196,000 Hoosiers fought for the Union, including over 1,000 Black soldiers. Hoosiers fought in 308 battles in sixteen states and one territory. After the Civil War ended, the state government had a monument built to remember those who served. The 284-foot-tall Soldiers and Sailors Monument still stands in Monument Circle in downtown Indianapolis.

Indiana continued to be a farm state in the years after the Civil War. In 1869, Purdue University was founded to teach agriculture (the planting and growing of crops). New companies and factories also came to Indiana. In 1876, Eli Lilly opened a business in Indianapolis to make medicines. His company went on to make billions of dollars. In 1887, the five Ball brothers moved their glass jar–making business to Muncie. By 1900, the Ball Brothers Glass Manufacturing Company was the largest maker of fruit jars in the United States. The company was so successful that the brothers were able to use their money to found Ball State University and Ball Memorial Hospital. Today the Ball Corporation is no longer based in Indiana but the university and hospital remain.

In 1905, the United States Steel Corporation bought land near the south shore of Lake Michigan for a steel mill (a factory where steel is made). The company built a city for its workers and named it after one of US Steel's founders, Elbert H. Gary. By 1908, between five to six thousand people lived in Gary, most of whom worked for the steel mill.

In 1910, Sarah Walker moved her business to Indianapolis because Indiana was a center for manufacturing (the production of large amounts of goods in factories). She was known as Madam C.J. Walker, and her company made hair-care products for Black women. She also owned a beauty school. Several thousand Black women were her salespeople and sold her products around the country. Walker donated to charities and churches and supported Black musicians, artists, and actors. She also worked for the fair treatment of Black people and an end to racist violence.

Elwood Haynes was also an Indiana business owner. In the late 1800s, he invented a gas-powered automobile called The Pioneer and opened a factory in Kokomo to build it. His company was one of the first to make cars in the

United States. More carmakers opened factories in the state. By 1909, Indiana produced the second-highest number of cars in the country. Within ten years, nearly two hundred companies built cars or car parts in thirty Indiana towns.

Cars starred in a new event when the Indianapolis Motor Speedway was built in 1909. Carl G. Fisher, James Allison, Arthur Newby, and Frank Wheeler worked together to pay for an oval track where cars could be tested and raced. The cars only went about as fast as fifty-seven miles per hour during the first race, but the track's crushed rock and tar surface was slippery and dangerous. One driver crashed and died on the first day of racing. To make the track safer, it

was paved with more than three million bricks. Soon it was nicknamed the "Brickyard."

Fisher and his partners decided to hold a new, bigger race—one where drivers drove around the speedway for five hundred miles. The first Indianapolis 500 was held on May 30, 1911. Forty drivers raced in front of an audience of eighty thousand people. The Indianapolis 500 became a yearly event, but it wasn't the only Hoosier sporting tradition launched in the 1900s.

CHAPTER 3
Hoosier Hysteria

In 1914, World War I broke out as European countries fought each other. By 1917, the US government felt it had to enter the war. More than 135,000 Hoosiers served their country. Samuel Woodfill, who grew up near Madison, became one of Indiana's greatest war heroes when he defeated three enemy machine gun stations on his own. James Allison, one of the founders of the Indianapolis 500, felt it was wrong to hold the race during the war. Instead, the speedway was used to house, fix, and test American warplanes.

When the war ended in 1918, many Americans were ready to have fun. In 1920, a high school basketball team nicknamed the "Franklin Wonder Five" helped launch "Hoosier

Hysteria"—Indiana's fierce love of basketball. Franklin was a small town, but its basketball team won three state championships in a row! Fans from around the state came to see the Franklin Wonder Five play. After graduating, some of the players followed their coach to Franklin College, where they won two state college championships. Three of the Wonder Five and their coach were later named to the Indiana Basketball Hall of Fame.

In 1921, a professional basketball player from Indiana named Charles "Chuck" Taylor went to the Chicago office of the Converse shoe company to complain that his feet hurt. He suggested the company design a shoe just for basketball players. Converse did, and Taylor went to work for them. Later, Converse added Taylor's signature to their Converse All-Star shoes. "Chucks" became some of the bestselling shoes ever made. Converse All-Stars—complete with Chuck Taylor's printed

signature—are still sold today.

Even Hoosiers couldn't survive on basketball alone—they had to eat! Indiana companies that prepared and packed food grew. Workers canned fruits, vegetables, and more in 166 factories around the state. One company in Franklin packed 234,000 cans of corn in one day! Indiana

led the nation in canning pumpkin and baked beans. In 1921, the Taggart Baking Company introduced a prepackaged sliced white bread and named it Wonder Bread. Around the same time, a young man named Orville Redenbacher grew his first popping corn on an Indiana farm, sparking a lifelong career in popcorn.

Indiana's Popcorn King

Orville Redenbacher grew up on a farm in Brazil, Indiana. He grew his first popping corn when he was twelve years old. He sold it on the cob in fifty-pound bags to local stores. He saved some of the money to pay for college at Purdue University.

Starting in the 1940s, Redenbacher grew and sold popcorn developed by Purdue's plant scientists. He and his business partner Charles Bowman worked to make a lighter, fluffier popcorn. It took more than two million stalks of popping corn, but Redenbacher and Bowman finally did it. They called their new popcorn Red Bow—Red for Redenbacher, and Bow for Bowman.

Their company became one of the largest makers of popcorn in the Midwest, but they thought their popcorn might sell better across the United States with a different name. They decided to use

Redenbacher's name and picture.

Soon, Orville Redenbacher's popcorn was known across the country. Later, the business was sold to Conagra Foods. Conagra Brands still makes Orville Redenbacher's popcorn today. It's the number one microwave and kernel popcorn in the United States!

When the United States entered World War II in 1941, Indiana's food companies stepped up to feed American soldiers. The Fairmont Canning Company packed turkey and other meats to ship overseas. Stokely-Van Camp made pork and beans and sent candy. Orestes Canning Company —which later became Red Gold, Inc.—canned tomatoes for the troops.

New factories opened to make materials for the war. The Evansville Shipyard built one ship every four days. Allison Transmission in Indianapolis made three thousand aircraft per month! The Indianapolis 500 was canceled so that fuel and rubber could go to the war effort instead of into race cars. Around 338,000 Hoosier men and 118,000 women fought for their country.

At the time, many women worked at home, managing their households and raising children. Factories needed workers, though, so many women took jobs outside their homes for the first time. Black people also moved from the south to find work in Indiana in large numbers. When the war ended, Indiana manufacturing continued to boom, and it had lots of new workers to help it.

In 1954, tiny Milan High School only had 165 students. Its boys' basketball team played a Muncie high school nearly ten times its size for the state title. Milan won, and their victory became known as the "Milan Miracle." Later, their story inspired the movie *Hoosiers*. A year after Milan's win, future NBA star Oscar Robertson led the Crispus Attucks High School team to the state championship. Robertson and his team won again in 1956.

Even though the Crispus Attucks team won two state titles and was the first all-Black team in the United States to win a state championship, their victory was not widely celebrated like Milan's had been. Crispus Attucks was an all-Black

high school. Most Black high school students in Indianapolis had to go there, even if a white school was closer to their homes. At that time, Black people throughout the United States weren't allowed to use the same schools or businesses as white people. This is called segregation.

In the 1950s, Black Americans acted to end

segregation. In Indiana, Black activists worked against unfair laws. In 1965, the Indiana state government passed laws to guarantee fair and equal treatment for everyone. In Gary, eight thousand Black political leaders gathered for the first National Black Political Convention to work for change. Still, it took until the 1980s for some

Indianapolis schools to finally integrate.

Indiana looked to the future. A Subaru-Isuzu car factory brought new jobs to Lafayette in the late 1980s. In Indianapolis, a software company called Software Artistry Inc. was so successful that IBM bought it for $200 million in 1997. Software Artistry Inc.'s former owners invested some of the money into other Indiana technology companies. Businesses that made food and chemical products also added workers. In 1990, Indiana was the twenty-ninth fastest-growing state.

In Indianapolis, the Hoosier Dome stadium—then the home of the Indianapolis Colts—and the Indianapolis Convention Center needed to be able to hold more people and were expanded in the 1990s. The convention center grew again and doubled in size in the 2000s. The Hoosier Dome was replaced by Lucas Oil Stadium in 2008, and the city hosted the Super Bowl for the first time in 2012. In 2024, the population of seventy-three out of Indiana's ninety-two counties grew. It was the largest increase in new people to the state in more than fifteen years. More and more people wanted to call the Hoosier State home.

CHAPTER 4
The Great State of Indiana

Today, nearly seven million people live in Indiana. Its regions are mostly rural, but there are several urban areas. Indiana has just over ninety-four thousand farmers, but most Hoosiers live within thirty miles of one of its cities. Indianapolis has the most people, with a population of nearly nine hundred thousand. Fort Wayne, Evansville, Fishers, and South Bend are other large cities.

About twenty-five thousand Indigenous people make their homes in Indiana. The state has returned small amounts of the land that was taken from Indigenous people in the 1800s. One hundred and sixty-six acres of land near South Bend was given back to the Pokagon Band of Potawatomi in 2016. The Miami Nation reclaimed forty-five acres of land near Fort Wayne in 2024. It has walking trails, a fishing pond, and community vegetable gardens.

Agriculture brings in about $35.1 billion to the state. Indiana is part of the "Corn Belt" (midwestern states known for producing corn), and almost half of its farmland is used to grow corn. Indiana is the number one producer of popcorn, and over 20 percent of the nation's popcorn comes from the state. Plants aren't the only thing grown in Indiana. It's the largest producer of ducks in the United States!

The Hoosier State is also home to many businesses. It's been the leading steel-making state in the nation since 1975. Indiana is a top producer of medicines and medical devices. Elkhart is known as the "RV Capital of the World" because its companies make 80 percent of the world's recreational vehicles. One of the largest onshore wind farms in the world can also

be found in Indiana. Wind energy produces over 9 percent of the state's electricity.

Indiana is full of places to have fun. Indiana Dunes National Park near Lake Michigan covers sixteen thousand acres, and more than fifty miles of trails cross its sandy dunes. The Indiana Cave Trail takes visitors deep underground and includes four caves: Bluespring Caverns, Marengo Cave, Indiana Caverns, and Squire Boone Caverns. Around thirty million people visit Indianapolis every year, where they might visit the Children's Museum of Indianapolis, the world's largest. The Holiday World theme park in Santa Claus, Indiana, is also popular. The town post office receives more than twenty thousand letters written to Santa every year!

Basketball is still big in Indiana. The boys' high school state tournament has been held for more than one hundred years, and the girls' state championship has been held for fifty! Indiana

University's Assembly Hall holds more than seventeen thousand people, and millions have watched basketball games there since it was built in 1971. New basketball star Caitlin Clark plays for the Indiana Fever, the state's WNBA team.

But it's not all basketball, all the time. Every November, the football teams of Indiana University and Purdue University play each other for the Old Oaken Bucket. It's one of the oldest football trophies in the United States. The Colts have won the Super Bowl once since coming to Indianapolis—they also won once before, when they were based in Baltimore. Hoosier athletes are also Olympians. Swimmer Lilly King, who grew up in Evansville and swam for Indiana University, has six Olympic medals, including three gold. Sarah Hildebrandt became the second American woman in history to win two Olympic medals in wrestling when she won gold and bronze in 2024.

More than one hundred Indianapolis 500

races have taken place since the first one in 1911. Hundreds of thousands of fans go to the speedway to watch it every year, and millions more watch the race on TV. The speedway's brick track was paved over in 1961, but a three-foot strip of the original brick makes up the start/finish line. Some winning drivers and their team kiss the bricks after a win!

Indiana has also been important to music and

art. Richmond record company Gennett Records helped change American music. Jazz greats Louis Armstrong, King Oliver, Duke Ellington, and Jelly Roll Morton recorded albums there. In Gary, Michael Jackson, Janet Jackson, and their siblings grew up as a part of a musical family. Michael and four of his brothers first performed there as the Jackson Five. He went on to have the bestselling solo album of all time and broke many other sales records in music. Robert Clark also grew up in the state. Later, he changed his name to Robert Indiana. He helped make the art style known as pop art famous. His sculptures of the word *LOVE* can be found in over fifty cities around the world, including at the Indianapolis Museum of Art. Other Indiana museums include the Indiana State Museum and the Eiteljorg Museum of American Indians and Western Art.

People have lived in the Hoosier State for thousands of years. Today, it grows some of the

nation's food and makes its steel. Hoosiers across the state gather to cheer on their basketball teams, no matter how small. It's famous for the Indy 500, the largest single-day sporting event in the world. Whether you travel its crossroads or call it home, Indiana is a state like no other.

Indiana at a Glance

Statehood: 1816

Nickname: The Hoosier State

Abbreviation: IN

State Motto: The Crossroads of America

State Tree: Tulip tree

State Insect: Say's firefly

Capital: Indianapolis

Size: 36,361 square miles

Population: About 7 million

Famous People from Indiana: Tony Stewart (race car driver), Vivica A. Fox (actress), John Green (author), Kenneth "Babyface" Edmonds (singer, songwriter, record producer), Larry Bird (basketball player)

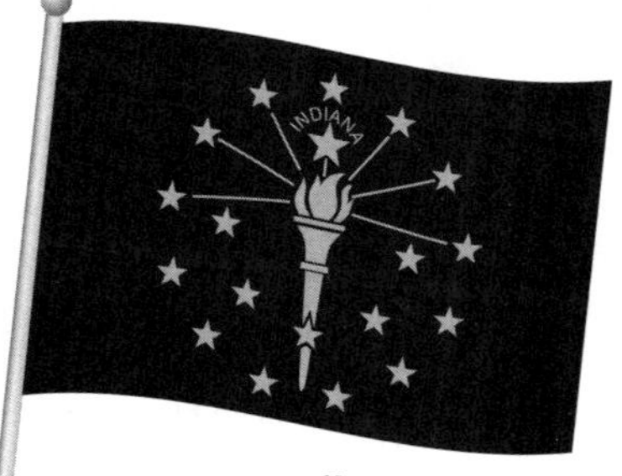

State flag

State bird

Northern cardinal

State flower

Peony

FUN FACT:

Six men from Indiana have been elected vice president of the United States.

Timeline of Indiana

1050–1450	The Mississippian people build Angel Mounds
1779	George Rogers Clark and his soldiers defeat the British near Vincennes in the Revolutionary War
1800	Indiana becomes a territory
1808	Tenskwatawa and Tecumseh build Prophet's Town
1816	Indiana becomes the nineteenth US state
1826–1846	Levi Coffin helps freedom seekers on the Underground Railroad
1876	Eli Lilly opens a company in Indianapolis
1906	The United States Steel Corporation builds Gary
1911	The first Indianapolis 500 race is held
1922	The "Franklin Wonder Five" win their third consecutive high school basketball championship
1944	The Evansville Shipyard makes one American ship every four days during World War II
1965	Orville Redenbacher and Charles Bowman make a lighter, fluffier popcorn
1971	Indiana University opens Assembly Hall
1990	Indiana is the twenty-ninth fastest-growing state
2024	The Miami Nation reclaims some of its land near Fort Wayne

Timeline of the World

1176	Construction begins on England's Old London Bridge
1778	England declares war on France after the French ally with the American colonies
1804	Napoleon Bonaparte becomes emperor of France
1811	The first all-women golf tournament is held in Scotland
1818	English author Mary Shelley publishes *Frankenstein*
1825	Russia and Great Britain agree to the boundary between Alaska and Canada
1845	The Great Potato Famine begins in Ireland
1876	The HMS *Challenger*, the first ship to study the deep sea, returns to England
1905	Scientist Albert Einstein publishes his first famous scientific theory
1920	Women in the United States gain the right to vote
1945	Seven Middle Eastern countries, including Egypt and Saudi Arabia, form an alliance called the Arab League
1962	Jamaica becomes an independent country
1971	The first email is sent
1990	The Hubble Space Telescope is launched
2024	Summer Olympics and Paralympics are hosted in Paris, France

Bibliography

***Books for young readers**

"Hoosier Facts and Fun." Indiana Historical Society. https://indianahistory.org/education/education-resources/educator-resources/fun-facts.

"Indiana." ***Britannica Kids***. https://kids.britannica.com/kids/article/Indiana/345482

"Indiana Pictures and Facts." ***National Geographic Kids***. https://kids.nationalgeographic.com/geography/states/article/indiana.

"Indiana: Quick Facts." ***Britannica Kids***. https://kids.britannica.com/kids/article/Indiana-Quick-Facts/630838.

*Pelkola, Elsa. ***Indiana***. Minneapolis: Abdo Publishing, 2023.

*Rathburn, Betsy. ***Indiana***. Minneapolis: Bellwether Media, 2022.